The Story of Autumn
A Golden Leaf

Rosie McCormick

an imprint of Hodder Children's Books

Text copyright © Rosie McCormick 2005

Design: Proof Books
Editor: Kirsty Hamilton

Published in Great Britain in 2005
by Hodder Wayland, an imprint of
Hodder Children's Books

The right of Rosie McCormick to be identified as the author of this Work has been asserted by her in accordance with the Copyright, Designs and Patents Act 1988

Apart from any fair dealing for the purposes of research or private study, or criticism or review, as permitted under the Copyright Designs & Patents Act 1988, this publication may only be reproduced, stored or transmitted, in any form, or by any means with prior permission in writing of the publishers or in the case of reprographic production in accordance with the terms of licences issued by the Copyright Licensing Agency

The publishers would like to thank the following for allowing us to reproduce their pictures in this book: Corbis: Ron Watts, title page; John M. Roberts 4; Raymond Gehman 7; Anne Griffths Belt 8-9; Roger Wilmshurst, Frank Lane Picture Agency 12; Matt Brown 14; Neil Miller, Paphilio 16; Joe McDonald 17; Lynda Richardson 18-19; Liu Liqun 21; Kevin R.Morris 22(bottom); W. Cody 23 / Hodder Wayland Picture Library: 3, 6 / Getty Images: Art Wolfe, The Image Bank 5; Steve Satushek Botanica 10; Yellow Dog Productions, The Image Bank 11; Jim Cummins, Taxi 13; Donna Day, Stone 1; David Young-Wolff, Stone 20.

British Library Cataloguing in Publication Data
McCormick, Rosie
A golden leaf : the story of autumn. - (The story of the seasons)
1. Autumn - Juvenile literature
I. Title
508.2

ISBN 07502 44313

Printed in China

Hodder Children's Books
A division of Hodder Headline Limited
338 Euston Road, London NW1 3BH

Contents

Changes everywhere	4
Stormy weather	6
Clouds above us	8
Puddles of fun	10
Carried away	12
A golden leaf	14
Surviving	16
The flight of the snow geese	18
Thank you!	20
The Hunting of the Great Bear	22
Glossary and index	24

Changes everywhere

As the warmth of the summer sun slowly fades away, the world around us begins to change. One season is almost over and another is about to begin.

In autumn, the evenings grow darker and the mornings cooler. The first glistening frosts cover the earth and green leaves turn to shades of gold, red and yellow. All around people, plants and animals begin to prepare for the cold winter months ahead.

5

Stormy weather

At this time of year, powerful autumn winds blow fiercely across land and sea. Trees bend and bow against such force and giant waves crash down upon the shores.

During the day, grey storm clouds darken the landscape. And at night, the sky is often filled with the sound of rolling thunder while lightning bursts upon the darkness.

Clouds above us

As summer disappears, clouds of different shapes and forms appear more regularly in the sky. Puffs of cotton, fluffy white sheets and feathery wisps of cloud are blown across the sky by the wind. Some clouds float high in the air while others are so low they almost touch the ground.

Watch out as dark clouds gather in the sky above you. Before long, rain is sure to fall heavily upon the earth.

Puddles of fun

The ground, rivers and streams are ready for autumn rainfall. Sometimes the land is parched and dry and the rivers and streams almost empty. Rain falls from the dark, thunderous clouds and revives the earth. Then it rises again as moisture to eventually form more angry rain clouds.

But after the rain clouds clear, you can put on your wellington boots and jump and splash in shimmering, sunlit puddles.

Carried away

All around nature is working its special magic. Plants are scattering their seeds so new ones can grow in the spring. Small seeds are swept up by the wind and carried to a new home. Ripe, juicy berries are eaten by animals and returned to the soil in their droppings.

Other claw-like seeds cling to animal fur and eventually fall to the ground. Waterside plants drop their seeds into the rivers and oceans, where they float away to a new place.

A golden leaf

Slowly, as the nights become longer and the days shorter, trees that shed their leaves get ready for winter. They no longer use the air, water and sunlight to make food. Instead they rest, and use stored up energy to survive until spring.

And so the leaves begin to die. Changing from green, to copper and gold before floating to the ground. The colourful leaves can be raked into soft piles of autumn fun.

Surviving

Some animals are able to live through the harsh autumn and winter months. To keep warm they may grow thicker fur. Animals, such as squirrels and mice, gather extra food and store it to eat later, while others eat different kinds of food as the seasons change.

But there are those that can't adapt. Instead they prepare a winter home. And there they sleep, safe and warm until the spring arrives.

The flight of the snow geese

As the autumn winds become bitterly cold, and food becomes harder to find, animals that cannot hibernate or survive the winter months set off on long journeys to far away winter homes. They migrate thousands of miles across land, water and sky.

Large flocks of snow geese leave their Arctic home and fly to a warmer place. They are guided by the stars, the winds and their own incredible instincts.

19

Thank you!

In autumn, before blankets of snow cover the ground, farmers gather ripe fruits, vegetables and grain.

For hundreds of years people have given thanks for the autumn harvest. In the United Kingdom, school children create beautiful harvest displays. And in America, on Thanksgiving Day, families come together to enjoy a special meal.

In China, people celebrate with lantern-lit feasts beneath a shimmering harvest moon.

The Hunting of the Great Bear

Why leaves change colour in autumn – a Native American tale

Once four brothers set off to hunt a great bear in autumn. The bear had large white teeth and red eyes. As it ran through the forests, trees crashed to the ground. The hunters were frightened but they did not give up. They followed the bear along a path that led up to a mountain top. There they caught and killed the bear.

The dead bear's blood dripped down upon the earth's forests colouring many leaves red. And as the hunters cooked the meat, fat dripped upon more leaves turning them yellow. When the brothers had eaten their fill, they looked about and realised that they were not on a mountain – but in the sky!

Glossary

Adapt – when something changes to suit a new situation

Energy – a force that makes things move

Frost – ice which forms on the ground on cold nights

Harvest – when ripened crops are gathered

Instinct – something we know without being taught

Migrate – when birds fly far away to avoid the winter

Moisture – water that is in the air or absorbed by something

Nature – all plants and animals

Season – spring, summer, autumn or winter

Seed – the small fruit of a plant which can grow into a new one

Survive – to live longer than other things

Index

bear 22
berries 12
clouds 6, 8, 10
frost 5
leaves 5, 14
harvest 20

hibernation 18
migration 18
rain 8
seeds 12
snow geese 18-19

storm 6
  – lightning 6
  – thunder 6
Thanksgiving 20
trees 6, 14
wind 6